ULTIMATE POET-TREE

SEMAJE TURNAGE

TURN OF AGES PRODUCTIONS
THE TIME IS NOW

The Ultimate Poet Tree

copyright@2021 by James Turnage and Andrea Flowers

Requests for information should be addressed to:626 Wilshire blvd suite 410, Los Angeles, CA 90017 semaje@turnofages.net

ISBN:978-1-5136-82969

Ultimate Poet Tree by James Turnage goes by Semaje Turnage

Summary : A collection of well crafted profound poetic words- by Semaje Turnage

Ultimate Poet Tree written by Semaje Turnage copyright @2021 Turn of Ages Productions, Inc.

ACKNOWLEDGEMENT

Thank God for blessing me with my talents and gifts. Thanks to my big beautiful family for all the love and support they gave and continue to give me. It brings me great joy to produce the Poet Tree Book and share the experience with them.

TABLE OF CONTENT

1. TO BE GOLDEN

Golden is to be of pure and uncompromising value. No matter what shape or condition, nothing can tarnish your essence. To be golden is to be a genuine character from the inside out, possessing perfect quality in the midst of imperfection, and having all impurities of the world brought to the surface and destroyed by the furnace of God's word. To be golden is to be refined, rejuvenated, replenished, and received by all were fascinating with its timeless beauty.

The Bible talks about the streets of Heaven being made of gold. It's God 's will for His children in having to walk on gold. Why is it that man feels the need to idolize, kill steal and deceive themselves for that which is under the feet of the children of the Most HIGH. His will be done on earth as it is in heaven and the righteous man's steps are ordered by the Lord. Each step of faith we take is a golden step leading us closer to our destiny. BE GOLDEN!

2. THE DRUG THAT MAN MADE

This is the drug that alters your brain known as cocaine that man made. This is the rock made from the drug that alters your brain known as cocaine that man made. This is the dealer who got the rock from the cop who went to Watts with the rock made from the drug that alters your brain known as cocaine that man made. This is the woman who sold her body to the dealer with the rock he got from the cop who went to Watts with the rock made from the drug that alters your brain known as cocaine that man made. This is the boy who hates his life, the son of the woman who sold her body to the dealer with the rock he got from the cop who went to Watts with the rock made from the drug that alters your brain known as cocaine that man made. These are the streets that taught the boy who hates his life, the son of the woman who sold her body to the dealer with the rock he got from the cop who went to Watts with the rock made from the drug that alters your brain known as cocaine that man made. This is the gang that claims the streets that taught the boy who hates his life, the son of the woman who sold her body to the dealer with the rock he got from the cop, who went to Watts with the rock made from the drug that alters you r brain known as cocaine that man made. These are the guns used by the gang, who claims the streets that taught the boy who hates his life, the son of the woman who sold her body to the dealer with the rock he got from the cop who went to Watts with the rock made from the drug that alters you r brain known as cocaine that man made.

These are the parents that lost their children due to the guns used by the gang that claims the streets that taught the boy who hates his life, the son of the woman who sold her body to the dealer with the rock he got from the cop, who went to Watts with the rock made from the drug that alters your brain known as cocaine that man made. This is the lawyer who prosecuted the thug who grieved the parents that lost their children due to the gun used by the gang who claims the streets that taught the boy who hates his life, the son of the woman who sold her body to the dealer with the rock he got from the cop who went to Watts with the rock made from the drug that alters your brain known as cocaine that man made. This is the judge who sniffs the drug, who knows the lawyer that prosecuted the thug who grieved the parents that lost their children due to the guns used by the gang that claims the streets that taught the boy who hates his life, the son of the woman sold her body to the dealer with the rock he got from the cop who went to Watts with the rock made from the drug that alters your brain known as cocaine that man made. This is the prison sentenced by the judge who sniffs the drug, who knows the lawyer that prosecuted the thug who grieved the parent that lost their children due to the gun used by the gang that claims the streets that taught the boy who hates his life, the son of the woman who sold her body to the dealer with the rock he got from the cop who went to Watts with the rock made from the drug that alters your   brain known as cocaine that man made. This is the free labor produced by the prison, sentenced by the judge who sniffs the drug, who knows the lawyer that prosecuted the thug, who grieved the parents that lost their children due to the guns used by the gang that claims the streets that taught the boy who hates his life, who is the son of the woman who sold her body to the dealer with the rock he got from the cop who went to Watts with the rock made from the drug that alters your brain, known as cocaine that man made.

There's a crack in the system that benefits from the labor, produced by the prison, sentenced by the judge, who sniffs the drug, who knows the lawyer that prosecuted the thug, who grieved the parents that lost their children due to the gun used by the gang that claims the streets, that taught the boy who hates his life, the son of the woman who sold her body to the dealer with the rock he got from the cop who went to Watts with the rock made from the drug that alters your brain known as cocaine that man made.

3. FREE THE CIRCUS LION

Born to be a king and claim his throne. The lion wears his crown with the mane it grows. He is the king of the Congo brave and bold. In his eyes is a fire with a flame that glows. But what happens when the lion is enslaved and sold. Stripped from his royalty and made to change his clothes. Whipped so many times until he's tamed and slowed. Isolated from the pride, locked, and caged alone. Taught to be domesticated not the ways of home.

If you try to set him free, he'd be afraid to go. Unnatural habitat shaped is dome. Mental winter entered center rain and snow. Drifting in the way and every which way it blows. No desire to hunt as they serve him prey in bowls. He's totally dependent until he's grey and old. Now ashamed of his name and he hates his own. Anything that resembles him is portrayed as foes. The Circus main attraction never paid what's owed. Kept in cages for ages and not made to know his heritage and where he comes from is paved with gold. Pressure made the diamond; it came from coal. Once he realizes who he is, he can break the mold. Be what he was created to be and take control. Who holds the ocean of emotion and the waves that flow. God 's eternal hard drive is what saves this soul. Start relying on the lion and create the show.

4. UNSTOPPABLE

Expand the land like lava from an active volcano, with the reverse impact of a massive tornado. No limit to what I can do and how far I can go, because I am unstoppable. Like the wings of an eagle, I will soar with the consistency of the ways that brush up against the shores.

When they think that I'm less, I know that I'm more, because I am unstoppable. Like the wind and rain every season when it changes, like the stars at night or the sunrise of a new day; like a runaway train, I can't be contained, because I am unstoppable. Intimidated by you? Not at all, because inside of me I got it all. I can turn dry places into waterfalls because I am unstoppable. Like a righteous prayer or Lawrence Taylor, the giant player. Like the words and deeds of our Lord and Savior, we are the salt of the earth, born to bring flavor, because we are unstoppable.

Like Michael Jordan, when the game was important, or the vibration of a good song that was recorded. You have to know that you are a champion before you are rewarded because you are unstoppable. Fail, I will not. I will learn and not get stopped. Keep moving like a clock on a wristwatch ...tick-tock. Do what you do for the love and not seek props. Turn the streets into gold like the art of hip-hop, because I am unstoppable.

5. POET'S TREE

Throughout America's history, the journey so far has been that of growing greatness with violent victories, a two-sided coin, one of pleasure and the other...misery. Sent the first man to the moon but that remains a mystery. In democracy's hypocrisy, we walk the board of monopoly. They control the paper, but we got the tree. Best known for legislation, education, and innovation. Domination, administrations with no limitations.

The declaration of the proclamation made it the nation of all nations. Master and slave separation with no reparations. Intimidation, discrimination, mental mass incarceration, isolation in the ghettos, modern-day plantations. The land of milk, silk quilts, honey, and money; where the impoverished person prospers to become king. From rags to royalty, that's how fertile the soil is. The dream is the seed we water with loyalty. It produces abundantly, the world wants to come and see. More goes on in private than what we see publicly. So what's the cure for the poor that some deem not worthy? The rich and needy coexist in the midst of controversy. As the world turned, the people learned and the sands of time began to rise, a new nucleus of people had a plan devised. While others chose to cry, riot, loot, and vandalize, the small group strategized, used faith, and the mind. Excuses were useless; they knew they could do it. Made the impossible possible, left the opposition clueless. The way society judged them they no longer cared.

The grizzly bear dares to compare himself to a polar bear. It was early morning, the sun rose and the path had been chose. As the wind comes and goes-where-nobody nobody knows. Like the fragrance from a rose, penetrating the nose. To rise we must first be low and that's how the tree grows.

In the tiny seed, we must believe in what could hardly be seen. Small beginnings, big results is what would be the theme. Underestimated, underrated but it's not what it seems. Potential is only hidden to those outside of the dream.

The universe is like an ocean, the conscious flow is the stream. Purified by the rain, change came to be clean. The dream is the seed pulled by the sun's beam. The tree that endures for sure, its leaves become green. So when we talk about faith, this is what we mean.

6. SALT OF THE EARTH

Going to bring forth life as the Salt of the earth. The highest form of creation, we are exalted from birth. What if the salt loses its taste? How will you be rated? Will it be hated because that's how we made it? Created to be sacred, but if you can't taste it, the essence of your salt, who can replace it?

Nothing on the earth because that's not the source. Can't take the salt from the sea or stop the force. Salt is better altogether not a grain at of time. A l flavor unit with a brain that's divine. Every grain working with the same purpose. Almighty God is stirring, so we're ready for serving. Every grain we rain with a common aim to change. We are all different but the same because of what we proclaim.

7. WRITTEN ON THE BRIX

Broken homes that provide no affection, so many are lost with no direction. Dope and alcohol shattered dreams like a bottle. Children joining gangs because of no role model. Graffiti field walls, drug dealers and violence, teen pregnancy, abortion, rape disease, and silence. Helicopters overhead, police have the wrong suspect. Low expectations run high in the midst of the projects. Bad is good, good is bad as people boast and brag. Rare to have a dad, so the neighborhood is sad. Mothers out of touch with reality, living a ghetto fantasy, intoxicated all day, and can't stand to see life through sober eyes as daily struggles increase.

Inner-city kids witness more war and peace. Incarceration and murder are considered a lifestyle, the pits of poverty are known to cover a bright child. Emotional wounds that need to heal, a hurt that gives birth to a need to kill. A shortage of love and overflow of hate, explains the ghetto mind state that causes a high crime rate. Low self-esteem and no motivation, we have to look inside ourselves and show the nation. You are what you believe, and I believe I can achieve. I am never going to give up as long as I can breathe.

8. GOODBYE YESTERDAY HELLO TODAY

If we do dwell on the past, how do we go on - pain back in the days locked in your bones? Trapped down memory lane and don't want to go, scared of the future because you know you're broke. Would have had it all a long time ago. When the sun sets the day did you know? Tomorrow is everlasting, yesterday's forever passing. Hurt, old as dirt, is why you're never laughing.

This was years ago but hurts like it just happens. Put your life in drive and stop reverse backtracking. Attacking you r emotions with the old sins. Excuses are useless and winners are going to win. Get up and face the pain. Break the chains of the past. Faith is forever present and shame doesn't last. You don't need a Time Machine to take you to a time or scene, just reminisce and it will hit you like a dream. Dreams are real only to the person who sleeps. Past pain only hurts the person who keeps it.

Whatever seeds you plant, best believe you reap. Sow no seeds and grow weeds, best believe you'll weep. Forgiveness is hard, but we got to learn to forgive. It's a commandment to all who believe that the Word is true.

9. THE NEST

What is the nest? The nest is where it all unfolds. It's what's hidden beneath the surface, and stories untold. It's the foundation starting line of nature's nursery. When we arrived in this life, the nest is what we first see. The nest is where we make our intro to begin our path; it's where we learn to love,

hate right, wrong good, and bad. It's a
safe haven where parents are supposed
to provide, give their young their best
chances to survive and thrive. The nest
is protection, a reflection of direction, a
place of development, support, and
connection. The nest is a blessing filled
with lessons and questions; ours is built
on oppress10n, aggression, and stress.
The nest is the soil where plants take
their root. Tears water the land and
cultivate the fruit. Of the bitter bushes
adorned with thorns, babies born with
the scorned nation's flag torn and worn.

Colors and streets define us, divide us, and ignite us. As law enforcement despises us, the judicial system chastises us. No passion, no purpose. I wonder where the desire went. Lost in the land of broken dreams, where we call our environment. This is a journey inside of Jim Crow's nest, made up of broken homes, drugs, guns, and farewell checks. Witness a real-life drama without any commercials as we look up in the sky and see the ghetto bird circle.

10. MASTER CREATOR

Where were you when the Word created the earth, made man from dirt, and gave water for thirst?

Do you know how the ocean waves roar u p to the shore and then go no more? Can you make the earth shake and listen to you? Does lightning and thunder need to get permission from you?

11. SELF WEALTH

Hocus bogus magically distracting me, got us 1magmmg catastrophe. They inflict nightmares to fulfill a fantasy while they take the fruit from my tree and actually sell it back to me. How can it be is the question you're asking me? The culture has been exploited by industries and factories. That which you desperately search for, you already have naturally. The best things in life are what we have for free, a relationship with GOD, love, friends and family, food, water, and shelter. So, just be glad to breathe. You are a piece of the Master, a work of art, and a Masterpiece.

NOW, in this very moment, is where victory is WON. It is not the past nor the future, but NOW, and only NOW, in the present, victory is WON .... The time is NOW ....

Semaje Turnage, CEO of Turn of Ages Production Company. Define today's Driven Young Filmmaker, Screenwriter, Poet, Author, Director and Motivational Speaker.

He recently completed writing multiples of Books, 2021: The Ghetto Bird's Nest" "Poet Tree", "Prisoner of Privilege", "Super Earth" and "Blacxodus"; Semaje has also written & directed five episodes of "The Ghetto Bird 's Nest" a hood dramatic series and pilot episode of "McClucky Fried Chicken" a comedy filmed both filmed in Los Angeles Ca, Semaje is a consummate Storyteller and a Passionate Poet. He lives and breathes the stories he creates that must be told. Even if there was no such thing as technology, he would be sitting around writing poetry orstories."

He also writes and composes the music for his productions, flavored with Hip Hop, R&B, Poetry and soul. Semaje company currently resides in Los Angeles, CA. In his spare time he is inspired to volunteer at detention centers and group homes as a Motivational Speaker. Semaje Turnage is truly an author with passion and purpose, which he boldly projects onto the screen through

his keen writing and solid direction.